THE PITCH

THE PITCH

EILEEN QUINN AND
JUDY COUNIHAN

CARTOONS BY BERGER AND WYSE

faber and faber

First published in 2006
by Faber and Faber Limited
3 Queen Square London WC1N 3AU

Typeset by Faber and Faber
Printed in England by Mackays of Chatham, plc

A CIP record for this book
is available from the British Library

ISBN 978-0-571-22741-9
ISBN 0-571-22741-4

2 4 6 8 10 9 7 5 3

Dedicated to Fernando Ghia and Jude Blau

Contents

Foreword

I am a film producer. I have been pitching film and TV projects to financiers for the past eighteen years. At first I absolutely hated it. Mostly, because I was nervous, I did it very badly. As time went on, I must have done it well from time to time, as I did manage to get a number of films made. I also had to listen to some pretty dire attempts at pitches from writers and directors trying to get me interested in producing their films. One guy pitched to me in 'real time', taking me scene by scene through the film – dialogue and sound effects included. Being English, I was too polite to interrupt, and sat for two and a half hours listening to his story of a paedophilia victim who committed matricide in order to run off with his step-father. Another pitcher told me the story of a man who tried to commit suicide twenty-five times. His droning voice had me contemplating my own suicide as the only rational means of escape.

So two years ago, when I schlepped along to Eileen Quinn's lecture, my attitude was slightly cynical. After all, you've either you've got it or not, right? Wrong. Hearing Eileen elaborate on the finer points of pitching creative material was my road-to-Damascus moment. As the lecture unfolded, I thought: *this is it, she's showing us how to build the bridge between art and money*. At last someone had managed to crystallise business common sense with practical pitching tips. She took no prisoners, letting no one, even the shyest of writers off the hook, all the while focusing on the direct correlation between pitching and the financing of creative material. The radical idea? We all have to do this thing – and it's easy.

The most important revelation for me was the simple breakdown of 'need to know' information that most buyers and financiers of film really want to hear in a pitch. It made total sense, supporting my own practical experience 'out there', and banished for ever my own residual nerves about going out to pitch. Since that first lecture I have watched Eileen's tools transform the blithering nonsense that all kinds of producers, writers and directors pass off as pitching into concise and enthralling sales pitches for films I might even go to see.

I saw an opportunity to bring this information to a wider audience: I decided to 'produce' Eileen's lecture into a book. We both knew from long experience that there is a distinct lack of information available about pitching and that most people hate doing it. Yet pitching a story is the beginning of everything. Who knows how many good stories have been lost simply because their creators couldn't pitch?

In the process I have interviewed many peers and colleagues from the UK and international entertainment industry. We've included their comments here not only to support the theories presented but also to illustrate or expand on some of the book's key points in the words of some great and seasoned filmmakers. I see this book as the portal through which creative people can pass into the murky world of films that actually get financed. This book and the tools within it will help shape a pitch so that the person sitting opposite will not yawn, fall asleep, interrupt or lose the will to live. In a business which is as precarious and challenging as it's ever been, it's a relief to be able to offer one guarantee: this works.

Pitching is not the whole endeavour. Knowledge and experience of the film business takes years to acquire and the learning process never stops. Also, no amount of craft or study can make a silk purse out of a sow's ear – there is no substitute for divine inspiration. But I now believe that learning to pitch well is the one thing anyone can achieve, and everyone should try.

Judy Counihan
London, 2005

ACT ONE

INSPIRATION

My first pitch

Fade in on two eyes full of abject fear.

I am standing at BBC reception in west London, new Pitching Shoes pinching my toes. My throat is so dry I can barely speak to the RECEPTIONIST when she barks, 'Name?' I wipe clammy palms surreptitiously on my trousers. 'Are you sure you're in the right building?' The right building? Oh God. What if they've forgotten I'm coming today?

It is 1989. My name is Eileen Quinn. I am a PRODUCER. I have come to my first pitch meeting, bearing a great idea for a TV drama. I haven't prepared anything except my outfit, and with seconds left to go, I am suddenly feeling very exposed. What happens next? What are the rules? Nobody tells you anything. There is a mystique about pitch meetings which the seasoned people refuse to dispel. It's our industry's Rites of Passage ritual – something you just have to go through, before moving on to the next level, bloodied but unbowed.

'Ooh, he's in a foul mood today,' confides the SECRETARY, who has arrived to escort me to her boss. 'Even for him!' she adds merrily. She leads me down endless long corridors, a labyrinth lined with ranks of firmly shut doors. 'Maybe I should drop breadcrumbs to find my way back,' I joke lamely. Somewhere in the distance I think I hear screaming. The odd greyish FUNCTIONARY scuttles by, clutching files and scripts, eyes down. A fluorescent tube above us sputters, sparks and goes dead. 'Here we are.' And she opens one of the doors without a flourish.

The EXECUTIVE is on the phone. 'No,' he's barking. 'Tell him for the hundredth time No – just tell him No, and I mean No. Fine. No – you just tell . . .' He looks over at me, making an apologetic gesture – just be a minute. I try to perch on the edge of the sofa, straining my calf muscles with the effort not to sink into the itchy fabric and disappear. The executive is speaking quietly and slowly, as if to an imbecile. 'I said . . . you tell him . . . no . . . this is the bloody BBC, right, and the answer is just N-O.' And he slowly puts down the phone. I am transfixed. 'Right,' he says, turning his weary face to me. 'So. Tell me about this project of yours.' And in that split second, I realise those 'no-no-no' missiles of his are now pointing right at me . . . and there's nowhere to run.

One

The Big Idea

Pitching is like conducting an autopsy before anyone's died. It's the reminder, if one were needed, that for some people film is an art and for others, it's an industry. Pitching is selling. Pitching is talking. Pitching is dating. Three things most writers do badly.
Anthony Minghella, writer/director, *Cold Mountain*

What exactly is pitching? It is 'selling the sizzle'. Convincing people of your creative idea before it becomes a reality. It is not unique to the entertainment industry. We all do it in our daily lives – whether we're trying to convince someone to go to a particular restaurant or watch something on TV, we are at it, all day long. You cannot escape being a buyer or a seller.

In the world of the Business we call 'Show', selling is absolutely central. What begins in the mind's eye as a tiny egg of an idea, fertilised only by time and imagination, has no chance of full gestation or birth unless it is sold on. I had a professor of English at university who stood up in front of us on day one of our Shakespeare class, holding the *Complete Works* aloft and then dashing it down on the floor. We were gripped. 'The *Complete Works*!' he scoffed. 'No such thing. Shakespeare's works are not "complete" until they are performed on stage for an audience!'

I often think of this when I am working with writers who don't want to – or believe they can't – pitch. If they don't master this simple art, then their idea will never become 'complete' – and certainly it has no chance of entertaining people for centuries to come. However many screenplays you have downloaded this week, and however beneficial that may be to your filmic education, they aren't complete works until they are filmed and screened to an audience. To begin with, they have to be PITCHED. And it's not only the writer who does it, of course. Here's how it goes:

The Pitching Food Chain

Once upon a time, a WRITER, alone in his garret room, had a Big Idea. 'Ping!' went the light bulb over his head, and 'Plonk!' went his fingers on to the computer keyboard. Later that night he told his WIFE all about it, waving his hands round and jumping up on a chair for the good bit. 'Brilliant!' she applauded. 'You have to tell your AGENT!' And the very next day he did just that. 'Brilliant,' cried the agent as soon as he heard it.'Great stuff! I must pitch it to a PRODUCER!' Who in turn pitches the DIRECTOR . . . who pitches the FINANCIER . . . who pitches the SALES AGENT . . . who pitches the DISTRIBUTOR . . . who pitches the MARKETING GUY, who pitches the EXHIBITOR . . . and on it goes, each one moving the story along the chain to the next. Until one fine day, you and I go along to the multiplex. We scan the marquee and the posters, which pitch the film to us, and we go to see the film – the very one that was once only a little ' Ping!' in a garret.

Whatever your place on that food chain, there are some common denominators to any pitch meeting. You are presenting a creative idea in such a way that the buyer can make three key decisions:

1. **Whether it ignites his interest (emotional connection)**
2. **Whether it suits his business needs at present (practical connection)**
3. **How much time/money he therefore wishes to invest**

In turn there are just two tools you bring to that meeting, the basis of all successful selling:

1. **Information gathering**
2. **Communication skills**

This book will show you how to master these tools, giving you the confidence required to sell your Big Ideas. Here you will find a series of principles about pitching. They aren't entirely my own. In fact, I've stolen most of them from selling experts in other industries – then adapted them to ours. These principles are not foolproof , but they are guides to progress. They won't make a bad idea good nor will they turn a unique idea into a formula. They will take the terror out of pitching for you, for good.

You may subscribe to that old adage that 'salesmen are born, not made'. This book aims to prove that wrong, to debunk the myths that keep so much talent hidden and so many good stories untold. A better adage for the novice pitcher is this: 'You have nothing to fear but fear itself'.

It's like everything – the more you do it, the better you get.
Stewart Till, Chairman, UIP

As an industry novice, I worked as Head of Development for Eric Fellner, a laconic, elegant young English producer who'd made his first feature, *Sid and Nancy*, at twenty-five. Today he runs Working Title, makers of *Four Weddings and a Funeral*, *Fargo*, *Billy Elliot*, *Bridget Jones* and many more. When I first went out to market my pitch, my training had come largely from a year of watching Eric do it. 'Just sit quietly,' he'd mutter, eyeing my Development Girl notebook with unease as the buyers approached. 'And don't say anything.' So I sat as instructed and watched him charm the investors. His pitching style was a unique and mesmerising kind of 'anti-sale', as baffling as it was effective. Delivered in a low monotone, laced with the odd wry smile and self-deprecating remark, this was the pitch of a man who did not sell, the pitching equivalent of the backhanded compliment. Why did it work? Perhaps because, like the bespoke shoes he stood up in, this style had a certain 'exclusivity' to it, as if to say, 'Maybe you'd like to join my small circle of associates, who appreciate this fine work.' It looked pretty good to me.

However, I was nothing like Eric – I was, and still am, an exuberant American enthusiast, a heart-on-sleeve optimist with a strong selling penchant inherited from my salesman father. One of my early pitch outings proved this – thankfully selling to someone I already knew, who I'd rung to tell I had 'the best project EVER and please could we meet?'

The day comes. I enter the executive sanctum and exchange some pleasantries. It being England, the weather almost certainly features as a topic. My enthusiasm to talk about a new thriller as a possible TV mini-series is palpable. I am, in fact, hugging the manuscript and hopping from foot to foot in

excitement. 'So tell me,' drawls the Executive, 'what are you so excited about then?'

As if touched by some unseen wand, I morph into Eric Fellner. My posture slumps, I cross my legs at the ankles and lean back, away from my listener. My voice is a low and laconic monotone. 'Well, it's a kind of thriller, you know, very complex, maybe you won't be interested . . .' The Executive squints at me through his cigarette smoke, clearly confused. 'Eileen, are you feeling okay?'

That day I learned a key pitching lesson: *to thine own self be true*. No point in pitching like someone else. You've got to find your own style, develop your own signature. When I began presenting 'The Pitch' as a lecture, I'd step out and ask for an audience volunteer. That wakes everybody up. 'Come on, I need a nice BIG man . . .' I'd purr. And up would come some large and hapless screenwriter. 'Now I'd like you to put this on . . .' I'd continue, while slowly unzipping my fitted Italian red leather jacket. And, of course, the poor guinea-pig would gamely try for a moment, maybe fitting half a forearm into the sleeve before I whipped it back in concern for its life.

I was making a visual point for a visual medium – they'd remember that big fellow struggling into my red leather jacket. I explained that I really wasn't there to make him pitch like me, any more than I was there to make my jacket fit him. In fact, what I aim to do is make the pitcher comfortable as himself, in any pitch situation.

There are no tricks to pitching. One should only be oneself. I know producers who jump up on a desk and act out every role in the story they are trying to sell. I myself, simply and

briefly, in straight-ahead fashion, tell my story, plus why I believe in it.
Larry Turman, Producer, *The Graduate*

Two

In The Beginning

Not long after those early pitching days, I was asked to do a 'little talk' about pitching for an industry group in Scotland. 'Come along and tell us some stories,' they said, adding with amazement, 'We heard you actually LIKE to pitch!'

At Heathrow Airport, waiting to depart, I had the epiphany which set me on the road to writing this book. I was standing at the bookstall, flicking through the pages of the movie magazines, when I saw out of the corner of my eye a weird little group. Three or four men, all wearing similarly ill-fitting brown suits, were poring over a specialist shelf of books. Not pornography, not cars or gadgets . . . but Sales. SEVEN TIPS TO SUCCESSFUL SALES! CLOSING THAT DEAL! SELL YOUR SOUL! All the books seemed to have a surfeit of exclamation marks on the cover, as well as a nasty picture of a grimacing executive looking not unlike the brown-suited boys: 'Bob Jones will tell YOU his SECRETS!' I shuddered to think.

But I was curious, so I wandered over. I picked up one of these books and had a little scan. Interesting. *I can use this*, I thought. That particular book – and this is true of most sales manuals – was full of acronyms. AIDA is one of the most famous: those of you who have seen David Mamet's *Glengarry Glen Ross* will remember it well. It goes like this:

A: attract the buyer's ATTENTION!
I: generate INTEREST!
D: create DESIRE!
A: tell them the ACTION you want them to take!

Easy, I thought. I scooped up a few of these tomes and headed for my pitch lecture, armed and dangerous. I made up my own acronym: PACT. This happens to be the name of the UK trade association for independent producers. Neatly, it's also a word that sums up the buying-selling transaction: a pact is a contract. Now I just had to think of the words to fit. What did I think were the crucial elements to a perfect pitch?

The single most important attribute for pitching a project is passion. If you don't believe in your film one hundred per cent, and convey that total belief to me, then I am not even going to read it, let alone invest millions of pounds in it.
Eric Fellner, Co-Chairman, Working Title Films

The PACT Test

I offered this up to the audience as a kind of 'checklist' before they decided what and when to pitch:

P is for PASSION. No doubt about it, top of the agenda – do you love your project (enough to spend two, three, maybe twenty years with it?) and think it *demands* to be done? If you are the writer, is this 'the one' that you are burning to write NOW?

A is for AUDIENCE. Ask yourself: who is your audience? Also, what do you know about your immediate 'pitchee' – about who he's got to pitch on to, and who is his ideal audience (market)?

C is for CLARITY. Can you play your story's melody? Not all the detail, not the harmony, but the bare bones of it, enough to get across its value without boring or confusing your listener?

T is for TENACITY. My personal favourite: are you tough enough to take all the rejection, are you prepared to fight and fight for your film to get made, pitch after depressing pitch meeting? Do you also know when to quit?

There, I thought. Done. That's my pitch lecture. But en route home, I knew I still hadn't armed the audience to pitch. So I set off once more, back to the selling experts, looking for the tools which would make a real difference – helping people to pitch better, and go on to make a sale.

Since then, I have put together a thoroughly practical lecture, adding material and honing it as I've gone along. Over the last twelve years, I have presented it to hundreds of writers, producers, executives, agents and directors across the UK and Europe. During that time I continued to produce drama and run an independent production company; I was therefore able to apply my own theories as a practitioner on a weekly if not daily basis. By presenting this material to such diverse audiences, I've also been able to canvass them – buyers and sellers alike – to acquire more insight into the universal challenges of The Pitch.

What has evolved is a kind of road map through the pitch process. Its starting point is still a diagnostic test (and PACT also remains a useful tool), taken from those who have proven their skill in backing ideas that make money. We then move into the vital process of preparing for the pitch meeting itself, looking at 'homework' you can do, as well as some observations about buyers at every level. We'll also go through some do's and don'ts for preparing yourself and your pitch team – and crucially, we will show you how to prepare the material in such a way that your story is clear when you enter the pitch arena.

Suited and booted, we then move down the road to a virtual tour around the actual meeting room, investigating the rhythms and structure of the average pitch meeting, and thus demystifying that rite of passage. And finally, we'll consider what to do if you can't get into the meeting, including the art of writing a pitch letter. My aim is that, by the end of the journey, you will be far better armed than I was at that first terrible pitch meeting all those years ago. However negative or busy or difficult your buyer, you will be ready and able to take him (or her) on, fully equipped to put your best foot forward.

Three

Showbiz

'This is show business not show friends'
Jerry Maguire

When I started out in the industry in Britain nearly two decades ago, I noticed that Art and Money were separated at birth. In the case of institutions such as the BBC, the people who looked after the art (programme ideas, design) and the people who looked after the money (contracts, sales) were even housed in different buildings, as if to underscore the point. Not only that, it seemed to be a 'business' built on friendship, where a small and élite group commissioned scripts and films from old university buddies, which they wanted to watch. In other words, not a particularly market-driven business. The American notion that audience research, demographic focus groups and test screenings were a vital part of the creative process, that a film idea had to be first and foremost economically viable, was indeed foreign. Over the years, this attitude has changed. A great factor in this shift has been the rising cost of making films – the more the risk, the greater the business acumen required.

'Pitch' is a deceptive word, really. It sounds like something you do in a baseball game, or perhaps it may conjure up a strip of green grass, men in white and summer picnics while you watch the cricket; in other words, fun – nothing too serious. Yet when you are pitching a film you are essentially asking someone for MILLIONS OF DOLLARS. The global film market today is worth $65 billion. That is equivalent to the GNP of the United Arab Emirates. Serious money.

I have a process I use to decide if I want to produce a given project; you may have a similar filter. Mine is:

1. Do I love it?(passion)
2. Can I envisage a finance plan for it, even if it's just an idea? Is there a market? Can we make money?
3. Is life too short? (nightmare talent involved, lots of co-producers or turnaround costs attached, etc)

If any film idea fails to satisfy the above criteria, I don't take it on.

It occurred to me that everyone probably does this. So I began asking some corporate investors, people who daily commit millions of dollars to major projects in the 'real world', what *their* criteria are for buying decisions. After talking to property moguls, venture capitalists and other so-called 'non-creative' (but deeply prosperous) types, I distilled the following key criteria – all of which can be applied to the pitch process in our industry.

The Investor Quiz

'What's in it for me?'
Some call this a 'good risk/return ratio'. If I put in a million,

what are the chances of making more than that? Why should I do this rather than keep my money in a building society? How large is the risk relative to the potential upside? What are you offering me as an incentive to invest?

You might argue that these questions are nigh-on impossible to answer in the nebulous world of creativity. Who knows if a film will work? So many failures have come from 'sure-thing' packages, and so many surprise hits have come out of nowhere. What the investor is asking for here is not a guarantee. He simply wants to know whether his risk is commensurate with the potential return he *may* get. *He who risks more gets more* is the guiding principle here. For example, if you are a screenwriter prepared to write your film for the producer/buyer 'on spec' (for free), then the buyer cannot expect to keep all of the downstream benefit, which will be a combination of fees/profit and creative control. Many writers and artists have learned to barter on that basis, turning the notion of risk/return ratio to their own long-term advantage. However, if the buyer is putting up a large fee for the writing of your script, you can reasonably expect to sign over the rights to him for a longish period, and he can reasonably retain the lion's share of fees, profits and creative control down the line. His risk is that there will be no film – that your creative efforts will not bear fruit. His reward for taking that risk is making money if he's backed a winner. Yes, it's a gamble, but because – once in a while – the rate of return can be so huge in our industry, many will take it. Our buyers, more than most, are gamblers.

'What's so special about this?'
Is there something innovative about this idea? In marketing

speak, what are the Unique – and sustainable – Selling Points of your project for the buyer? In the world of property invest-ment, for example, the selling point is very often the location of the property. In the world of big business, a USP may be that the investment opens up a new market or client. How might this be translated to films? Selling experts commonly say, 'We buy with our hearts and rationalise with our heads' – so part of the USP has to be that the project 'touches' the buyer in some way , and of course it must also relate to his market and current needs. We'll go into this in more detail later, when we deal with pitch preparation for your specific project, but suffice it to say that if a film idea does not have a unique quality, then the investor will be hard pressed to believe that this is a must-have project.

When being pitched, I have an implicit underlying question that I would like to see (or hear) answered:'Why is this script different from all the other scripts?' Why, among the dozens of scripts I COULD read, should I read THIS one?
Tony Safford, Senior Vice President, Twentieth Century Fox

'Who's in charge?'
The management team of a company is profiled on the first page of any good business plan. Why shouldn't this apply to the proposition for making a film? If a youngster approached a bank for investment in a start-up business – say, running sandwiches around office buildings – the loan they receive will be small: it's a modest enterprise for a person with little track record. But the bank would still want to know what his education and experience was, and will probably ask if his parents can countersign the loan. In film, the investor will

also want security if the creative team doesn't have much track record. It may well be the security tied to the intellectual property (i.e. the copyright material you own, such as the book or script upon which your film is based). It could also include the addition to your novice team of a seasoned 'parent' – a mentor or an executive producer who can help steer your ship to safe harbour. They will also want to see how you and your 'management team' respond to criticism and feedback in the pitch meeting – start as you mean to go on. Above all, they will be looking hard at the director: however new, they must inspire confidence – they are 'the captain of the set'.

'What's it worth?'

I tried to sell my house recently, and was advised to get three or four estate agents in to value it before choosing one. The first three that I invited to view all pitched for the business, with quite a wide variance in asking price and commission rates. I felt a bit nervous about the one who told me it was worth far more than I had thought, and somewhat aggrieved by the fellow who told me it would sell for much less. Then along came the fourth. By this time I was fed up with the pre-liminaries, so before we'd even got to the attractive off-street parking with planning permission opportunities, I blurted out, 'Well, what's it worth?' He turned to me and smiled. 'It is worth what someone will pay for it.'

The same principle applies to films. Sensible pricing is vital. It relates, of course, to the risk/return ratio equation above. How much is someone – and I don't just mean the actual film financier – prepared to pay for your film? The answer is another question: what is the market prepared to pay for the film? This is where sales estimates come in, and why they play such a vital part in the film financing process. Based on a number of relatively scientific factors – primarily, what else has sold lately in a similar vein – sales agents can prepare actual forecasts of your film's profits in today's market (with a range of high, low and median sales not unlike my clutch of estate agents). It is wise to pitch your film at the low to median level of Market Value, rather than taking the (all-too-common) approach, 'I need this much money to realise my vision'. The latter is a good way *not* to make a movie.

I have been asked to make very big-budget films in Hollywood, but I know I can go back to Brazil and make two to five-million-dollar films. So, for example, I didn't have a director's chair or a trailer because these things are superfluous. I don't want to get used to the paraphernalia. Keep it light in your head, that is my advice.
Walter Salles, Director, *The Motorcycle Diaries*

Finally comes the consensus, the most important investment 'incentive' or criterion of all:

'Is this a once-in-a-lifetime chance?'
Everyone, however jaded or rich, wants to believe they are getting in on the ground floor of some project which is an exceptional opportunity. Why? For some, it may be because they have such a fat portfolio and such a lot of money that the hassle involved in taking up a new enterprise really must be matched by the sheer excitement involved. For others, it may be that they have limited resources and thus want to choose

with tremendous care since they cannot spread their investments across a wide range of opportunities. Some will have the 'once-in-a-lifetime' hit of their competitors firmly in mind: 'I want my own *Four Weddings*.' And for many, it is a very human instinct, linked to ego: they want to walk along the river and point to that remarkable new building and say, 'I made that happen.' This is acutely true of film financiers, because entertainment is such a long-armed beast. For the guy who invested in, let's say, *The Full Monty*, there must be a great deal of pleasure on his balance sheet each year – but there's also sheer human pleasure in knowing he can get into a cab anywhere in the western world and when the cabbie says, 'What do you do?' he can reply, 'I am the man who brought you *The Full Monty*.'

Some might argue, as with risk/return assessment, 'Yes, but the guy who green-lit that little British story could not have known at the point of purchase that this was an exceptional, once-in-a-lifetime decision!' This is where we move out of science and into the realm of instinct. A wise and skilful investor may just have a 'feeling' about a film (or an office block, or signing a particular musician to his record label) when he decides a particular opportunity is remarkable. This is known as the buyer's 'leap of faith'. Remember, the key factor to enable that leap is that *it feels remarkable to HIM* – not to you. So the producer of *The Full Monty* would not have made his sale by saying, 'I bring you this film – which is my first-ever comedy, a once-in-a-lifetime experience for me and the director'. He would more likely be saying, 'I bring you a chance to invest, at very little risk due to our low budget, in a feel-good, universal British comedy.' And to a Hollywood studio (in this case Twentieth Century Fox), that must have felt pretty exceptional.

Let's apply these key criteria to another British film success story, *Four Weddings and a Funeral*:

Risk return. Low cost (£2.9 million): the budget was low and all the world rights were available for the investor (Polygram) to take up. In the end it grossed over $250 million worldwide.

USPs. This was a romantic comedy capitalising on two strong features of contemporary life well known across the globe: the commitment-phobe male and the cliché of British high society. Also, it was the first film of a successful, award-winning TV writer, with a role for an American female lead. And it had an arresting opening: one of the financiers still talks about the memorable first few pages, which featured the word 'fuck' as the only dialogue!

Strong management. Track record of Duncan Kenworthy, an established producer, and Mike Newell, an experienced director (though he did not have a track record in film comedy as such).

Sensible pricing. The original budget was £3.2 million, but they couldn't get it financed at that level. With deferrals and cuts they reduced it to £2.9 million, and managed to get more finance when they attracted Andie McDowell to the cast.

Exceptional opportunity? A remarkably funny script which just might be the next *Fish Called Wanda* – this is how it was pitched.

Now let's apply this to YOUR film. Whatever project you are taking out to pitch in the near future, can you satisfy those investor criteria before you head out of the door? In a quiet room, ask a colleague or a friend to sit opposite you and ask you those five simple questions: the Investor Quiz.

Even if your buyer doesn't express his concerns in those exact words, you can count on the fact that someone down the line will want to have satisfying answers to all of the above. Try this exercise if you are having trouble. Switch chairs with your friend and YOU take on the role of the buyer. Ask those five questions, with the mantle of the businessman/buyer firmly wrapped round your shoulders. Having heard your pitch, can your friend answer? As you do this, you will fully understand that these questions are like probes or metal detectors, pushing across the sand hoping to ring out 'Eureka!'. This is how investors make their decisions. How does it feel to sit on the other side of the table?

ACT TWO

PREPARATION

Four

Step Up To Bat

You hit home runs not by chance but by preparation.
American baseball coach Yogi Berra

The day of the big pitch dawns. How is it for you? Are you lying in bed paralysed with fear, rehearsing the way it will go in your head? (This inevitably ends with the tragic words: 'Sorry, we already have something indirectly similar in development. Next!')

Maybe you are bouncing out of the house without a care in the world, shirt untucked and face unshaven, barely remembering you have a pitch meeting that day (in which case you are a writer, not a producer).

Or are you on the bus this morning, lips moving silently to your own special catechism, committed by rote to the twenty-five-word pitch you've heard they all do in LA. Is that you, lurching to the left and right as the commuters jostle, thinking, 'O God, was that twenty-five words or twenty-nine – gotta get this down'?

All of the above describe pitchers who are unprepared. Anyone entering a pitch meeting must be ready for it. This means preparation in three distinct areas.

1. The Buyer
2. Yourself
3. The Material

Preparing for the Buyer

The Golden Rule: he who has the gold makes the rules.
Anonymous

Time for some information gathering here. We're going on a whistle-stop tour of the Buyer's Psyche: his motives, desires and rules of thumb.

There's that old adage about public speaking, something I heard at school: when you get up on stage in assembly, quaking with nerves, just look out at the crowd before you . . . and imagine them naked. Of course, if you've ever tried this you will know that it's terrible advice. Imagine them naked? It's the most distracting idea, destined to doom you to stuttering failure. But underneath it is a perfectly good notion. Nakedness is vulnerability. Buyers are, by definition, vulnerable. If they don't buy well, they lose their jobs. Vulnerability manifests itself in certain behaviours and signals certain fears. The more we understand these, the better chance we have of making a sale.

Again I went back to the bookshop, to those shelves filled with colourful titles about deal-closing and selling strategies . . . and found a veritable treasure trove of material on Buyer Psychology. I began to strip out what was most useful for us pitchers. I have added to this overview by interviewing buyers in our industry, mixing and matching their insights with the conventional sales wisdom below. But first ask yourself some very basic questions about the type of individual you are going to see. Do you know the following?

> Age
> Pronunciation of name
> How he or she likes to be addressed
> Job title
> Credits (what have they done/made?)
> Gender
> Education
> Ethnicity
> Religion
> Health
> Marital status
> Dependents
> Attitudes/values/politics
> Lifestyle

Many new business pitches are lost because they were based on assumptions. Get the facts. I still wince when I remember a pitch meeting I had with a middle-aged man who I knew was married and just 'assumed' had kids. My film was about a woman whose son goes missing. 'You know how it is as a parent...' I began – and he interrupted coldly, 'No, I don't, actually.' There was little I could do to retrieve the situation.

So, ask around, find out as much as you can from others who have met him, surf the internet, read the trades, hoover up as much detail, large or small, about the buyer as you possibly can. Try to dig up one-to-one interviews with your buyer. I tend to clip and save all interviews with potential buyers published in the trades, even if I know them well, keeping them in an alphabetised accordion file in the office. I pull them out for a quick scan just to update myself before a new pitch meeting. You never know what small fact or figure can help you to gain insight and therefore target a particular project at your buyer. The other good thing about profile-type interviews is that they commonly include a photo – if you don't know your buyer, it's wise to 'put a face to a name' before the meeting.

Having established the externals, you are ready to step inside their psyche – and look at them naked.

Fears All Buyers Have

The best advice about taking on an enemy in wartime – or a buyer at market time – is to 'banish your fears by knowing theirs'. It seems that all buyers share one common fear, known in the trade as 'Buyer's Remorse'. I also like to call this phenomenon 'post-consumer tristesse'. Basically it's the sick feeling in the pit of your stomach after making a big purchase. It increases dramatically with the size of the investment.

How does knowing this help you to pitch? It may give you some sympathy for the buyer when he is hesitant or even aggressive; you will know that secretly he is afraid of making a commitment and then regretting it afterwards. This is useful in helping you not to take negative behaviour too personally – it's not solely because of you or the project, this is something ALL buyers experience to some degree.

Can your buyer get over this fear? If his needs are being met, you will quash the sense of impending remorse. Ensure your project meets the aforementioned key buyer criteria and that you have presented it so that the buyer knows it! If it satisfies those elemental needs, he's going to plunge on, happy to commit.

Buyers come in all shapes and sizes. (They are also as often women as they are men these days. I use 'he' for shorthand only). It's hard in our industry simply to file everyone under 'The Buyer'. The first thing which may strike you in the pitch arena, and it is deceptive in its unimportance, is nationality.

When it comes to pitching, Americans seem to have an extra gene . . . Salesmanship! Whether it is a used car, script, or idea for a film, they know no shame.
Sandy Lieberson, Producer/Chairman of Film London

The northern European tradition of self-righteous modesty is contradictory to even entering a pitching session. Our tradition for criticism or simply silence is stronger.
Lone Scherfig, Director, *Italian for Beginners*

Whether buying or selling, cultural differences are often a concern. Without doubt different nationalities and their respective industries have particular nuances and foibles:

Americans are seen as natural salesmen, continental Europeans are less concerned with genre than visual style, the Brits are more writer-led than other buyers, and so on. Don't let that confuse you too much. Be true to yourself and your story in front of any buyer. Remember this: no matter where they hail from, scratch the surface and buyers everywhere have much in common. I believe age and experience are better barometers than nationality for measuring buyer behaviour and reactions.

The Three Ages of Buyers: A Rough Guide

There will more than likely be a development assistant in the room, taking notes as you pitch. Be sure to acknowledge and engage this person before, during and after your pitch. Aside from being good for your soul, it's also smart – that person can influence the executive's impressions of you and your project.
Ron Parker, US TV writer (*Nuremberg, Joan of Arc*)

YOUNG BUYERS, also commonly known as 'collectors' in sales parlance, have neither authority nor influence, but act as a conduit, collecting information and material. They are often female and dismissively (or fondly) known as D-Girls. This is basically an entry-level job. They sound irrelevant, don't they? But they are not: from the bottom of their expensive shoes to the top of their highlighted heads, these pawns are very important to pitchers – because they may be the first, and possibly the only, buyers you get to meet. Your rapport with them is essential. What do they fear most? *That the wrong decision (or recommendation, since they are rarely able to make investment decisions) will ruin their career*. This can paralyse them. Years ago I had a great notion that I'd stop sending scripts to the big cheeses in the film world, who clearly never opened their post and didn't read anything. No, I'd pitch to the little guys, those D-Boys and D-Girls who are so full of beans that they'd be sure to jump up and down and champion my script right up to the top table. It seemed like a good plan – but I was wrong. Young buyers don't reply, they don't act – because any move will either reveal them as a fool with no power at all, or an underling with poor judgment. The best way to allay their fear is by playing to what you know about their boss. I think of this as a relay race. You are handing that D-girl your project. You are coaching her, you are metaphorically rubbing her shoulders and patting her on the back, to take that baton up the line, for her own benefit as much as yours: the message you must convey (with sound supporting reasons!) is that crossing the finishing line will please her boss.

Let's move on to your AMBITIOUS MID-RANGE BUYERS or 'key influencers'. They have influence but no authority. However, their influence is very strong. They might be a Commissioning Executive in television, or an Independent Producer in film. They are a man (or a woman) with a track record, who wants to go further fast. What they fear most is *losing face*. Such buyers are afraid that a bad choice will diminish any esteem or success they have gained so far. They care about what other people think, and your pitch must take that into account. Here the pitcher needs to present the material in such a way that your buyer can see how it builds on his existing success. I once pitched an idea by fanning out four imaginary aces – the first three were to represent films my buyer had already made, the fourth was the film I had just pitched to him. I could make a reasonable case that it complemented his work to date, and added strength to his portfolio. It also met his basic investment needs quite well – but what I was really doing here was indicating to him in code: 'Look, you aren't going out on a limb into some strange area that will make people wonder about you. This makes sense for you – and whether it's a hit or not, everyone will understand why you invested. Ergo, you will not lose face.' I remember reading a great interview with Henry Kissinger years ago where he talked about why the West always failed in its negotiations with the East: it was because we didn't understand that in their culture, they must above all else not lose face. The same is true of this key buyer, to whom you are going to be pitching more often than not.

Finally we come to the DECISION MAKER, also known as 'The Man' (not because he's male – it's another classic sales acronym for 'the person with the Money, Authority and Need'). This fellow doesn't give a damn what others think about him any more. He's got a row of prizes on his shelf; he's got three phones ringing, three movies shooting and three ex-wives. He's rarely paralysed and he's not interested in esteem. But he's still got one big fear: experience has taught him that he can be wrong. So he's afraid, in the words of William Goldman, that 'nobody knows anything'. What if he's dismissing the Next Big Thing? What if he's passing on *The Full Monty* (as every single film Decision Maker in Britain did)?

He's at the top of the tree because he's often been right, but at the back of his mind is that little nagging doubt. What if . . . I'm wrong? You can take advantage of this. Generally, towards the end of a short meeting (they are all short with Top Buyers, they've learned to budget their time – just as meetings with D-Girls are often ridiculously long), if they seem to be dismissive, you can grab their coat tails and pull. If they give you the right grounds, politely remind them of a similar project that might have sounded unlikely on paper but made a lot of money for the financier. Without saying it outright, this taps into that 'nobody knows anything' fear and may just sway him.

Negative Assumptions

Buyers far and wide readily admit to certain negative assumptions when a pitch commences, whether you are selling motor cars, office supplies or film scripts. If you know what these are, you may be able to surprise your buyer – and in doing so, delight him. While his guard is down and he's well disposed towards you, you are edging closer to a sale.

Their time is more important than yours.

Hence the amount of rescheduling and cancellation by buyers. Over the years I have set a Rule of Three for myself: if they cancel three times, then the meeting's going to be bad anyway – and do you want to make a film with someone who is so stressed and so rude?

They expect you to try and 'close' the deal.

I aim to surprise my buyers by NOT trying to close. I don't

ask them for a decision that day. Sometimes, if appropriate, I start by saying, 'I haven't come here today to sell you anything' (that old trick), or I might even show them my bag and say, 'Look, no scripts! Just wanted to sound you out on a few things.' This sets them at their ease, especially in Britain, where we seem to hate buying almost as much as we hate selling.

They think buying right away is losing.
Even if the pitchee LOVES your project, he's very unlikely to let on straightaway. The evidence is that this is truer in the UK and Europe than in the USA – the Americans beat us hands-down on follow-up and response time. Part of the reason for this is that projects are often 'auctioned' in the supermarket that is Hollywood, with 'hot' scripts sent out for multiple 'weekend reads' by film executives. In boutique Britain we tend to have a more timid and polite 'house-to-house survey' approach, which means that pitch and response activity can take years off your life.

They believe it is okay to lie to you.
In fact, Yes can very often mean No, which is confusing. If you know this when you go in, it will diminish the disappointment you experience out there in Pitchland. I once heard of an executive who was always pleasant and warm to his supplicants, but had three buttons wired up underneath his desk, which communicated secretly to the outer office. Number One meant 'interrupt me in five minutes with an urgent call and get rid of this guy'; Number Two meant 'after fifteen minutes, come in and remind me my next guest is about to

arrive'; and Number Three meant 'pop your head round the door in half an hour and say "your car's here"'. The moral of the story is: watch your buyer's under-desk movements . . . and try to not take him at face value.

It is always important to give the courtesy of undivided attention to a pitch. That way there is no guilt when you pass the next day.
Russell Schwartz, President, New Line Cinema

Before you become completely depressed by these observations, it is important to remind yourself that the buyer's job is, in fact, to BUY. He needs you just as much as you need him, because if all he really did was cancel meetings and press those bad buttons, he wouldn't have any projects to make/distribute/broadcast. That's why he sits through all those hundreds of pitch meetings: some of them are going to bear fruit. Once he gets past his negative assumptions and fears (with your help!), he is ready to get down to business. This usually involves asking you *questions* about your project.

QUESTIONING is the heart and soul of any sales meeting. You might think that all questions should come from the buyer – and many will. But every pitch meeting is also a golden opportunity for you to ask questions, and this can be a surprisingly effective route to sales success. But let's start with the buyers.

Having interviewed numerous buyers and sellers over the years, I have produced a shortlist of Commonly Asked Buyer Questions in Pitch Meetings. As I learn more, I am always refining and making additions to it – although it is remarkable how consistent the list is, no matter what country you are in, whatever the project or the size of the company. Any experienced pitcher will recognise at least half of these questions from his most recent pitch meeting. And novice pitchers are certainly going to hear them in the years to come. Make sure you can answer all these questions about your first or next project going out to market.

Commonly Asked Buyer Questions

Would you like a cup of coffee?
Stewart Till, Chairman, UIP

What other films is it like?
(Variations include: 'Who is the film's audience?'; 'What shelf would it sit on in the video shop?'; 'Where would it sit in the TV schedule?'; 'What cinema would it play in?') They are asking about the film's 'relatives', its brothers, parents, cousins and grandparents. They are certainly NOT asking you to launch into an 'X meets X pitch'. They really want the comfort of knowing that people have gone to see other films somehow 'like' yours – it provides security. You may feel that your film is totally unique, and you can say so – but in that case be ready to explain how it might add value to the buyer's business.

Why should we identify with the hero?
('Whose story is it?'; 'What's it *about*?') It helps to tell the story from your hero's point of view. Can you show the buyer the universal connection a large audience can make with the hero? In other words, does he want something or reveal

something in the course of the action that has meaning for the audience?

Why now?
('How is it relevant today?') Often asked about period material, especially if it is set in the recent past (the 1980s, for example). Underlying this question is concern about whether today's audience will watch it.

Why is it a feature film and not TV?
Commonly asked in Britain and Europe, where the two industries cross over, feeding each other financially and creatively. If you are pitching a feature, you'd better have a strong answer. This is a real party game in our industry: what makes a story a film and not TV? My own answer is that a feature film has to have qualities that are persuasive enough to get me out of my house on a dark and rainy night and to pay the babysitter/parking/popcorn/ticket etc. In other words, it has to have a 'must-see' quality about it, or I'll just wait for the DVD, stay in and watch some telly. It could just be that the film in question 'has a big star in it' or 'a big director' or 'a stunning visual landscape' (which I'd prefer to see on a big screen).

Why did you want to do this?
('How did you come to get involved?'; 'Why did you want to create it?') This is a vital but trick question. In replying, tell the truth, but also try to make the answer important for the buyer. They are really asking, 'Why should *I* want to do this?' You may have got involved because something like

this story happened to you in real life, for example, but the buyer doesn't care much about you. What about *him* and his audience?

What's the budget?
They aren't really asking for an exact figure, especially if you are only at idea stage. This is a question about ambition. Is it low, medium or high budget? Similar to what other recent film? Did they make that film? Is it in the budget range of movies that they tend to finance? Do your homework.

They are asking about director and cast. If it's far too early for either, this question may be a way of probing for a fuller sense of what 'size' film you aim to make – or it may be that they are struggling to get a mental picture of your leading characters. A bit of 'pie in the sky' casting helps that effort. This is not to be confused with lying about the actual talent attached.

What's the poster?
Most likely to be asked by a film sales agent or distributor, although I have known others to ask. Again, this is helping them to visualise what kind of look and style you have in mind for the film. It's not a question of mocking up a poster and bringing it to the pitch (although some people do, with great success) – it's about knowing what your big selling points are, as these would surely feature on any eventual poster. If you have a really fantastic 'logline' (poster tagline), this is the moment to trot it out. Think of *Jaws*, a film which came out over thirty years ago, and its still mem-

orable logline: 'Just when you thought it was safe to go back in the water . . .'

What happens at the end?

You'd be astonished how often this comes up. Why? Because so few pitchers get that far. They get lost in the plot details and the great opening and their USPs, and are commonly stopped half-way because their pitch has confused the buyer, who now needs to ask for some clarification. Or pitchers are coy about the ending, thinking that it will make the buyer desperate to read the script if they refuse to tell them how it ends. In my opinion, this is a mistake. The meaning of a film is vested in its ending: if the end sounds good, the buyer will be all the more interested to read your script. Remember, they don't just want to know the ending

out of curiosity – they want to know if the audience will feel satisfied by it. Where endings are concerned, a good exercise is: stand in front of the mirror, or a colleague, and be the main character in your film; say to yourself, 'In the end, I (the protagonist) learned/did . . . and this is important for the audience because . . .' If you can fill in those blanks and communicate this to the buyer, you're winning.

In a pitch, get to the story quickly. Let the story be told from the principal character's point of view, they are the camera and that is how the story is told. Make sure the story has a theme that reaches a conclusion.
Mike Medavoy, Chairman, Phoenix Pictures

After the pitch meeting, at the end of his long day, your buyer will sit at his desk and consider the many pitches he has heard. Maybe yours and a few others are interesting to him. He moves the bits of paper or script around on his desktop absently, like jigsaw puzzle pieces, wondering what he will do with them, if anything.

At this twilight hour, something very important is happening in his head, even if he's not fully conscious of it. He is rapidly prioritising which pitches stand a chance of going further. He has shortlisted them already, probably keeping a running tally during his day. Now he's going to rank them and consider what to do next. This process is called the 'purchase decision'. It's you in a shoe store, having tried on the blue, brown, and red pair, high and low heels, leather and suede. You are now thinking, 'Well, blue goes with a lot, but red is more fun, and suede gets ruined in the rain, but then I have a lot of leather already . . .'

Turning the Tables: Your Turn to Ask Questions

To really get inside that decision process, and learn enough about your buyer to ensure your project goes to the top of his pile before he leaves the office that night, it's vital to ask some questions. At a certain point in the pitch meeting, usually towards the end, you may get this opportunity – be ready to take it!

You can take various approaches to questioning the buyer directly. The worst question you can possibly ask him is, 'What are you looking for?' They usually just stare at you and reply, 'I'll know when I see it'. Below are some more effective lines of questioning.

Before you begin, remember this: the ability to listen to the answers is vital to your future success. Few salesmen are naturally good listeners. It is a core communication skill they have to practise. Some sales managers get team members to 'audit' each other, spending a day or a week noting how they are doing as listeners and then giving each other feedback. It can hurt, but it's a great exercise in humility – and in selling. Essentially, people who value others are good listeners – and effective pitchers.

The Pain Funnel

Best used when you know the buyer well and have a track record – it's inadvisable go through this with a total stranger.

This approach is very simple and can be used when time is short. It's a common sales tool which is uniquely well suited to our business, owing to what I'll call the Quinn Principle: *Everyone Likes to Moan*. In your own words, in the following order, you ask:

What's not working for you at the moment?
What are you doing about it?
How long have you been trying that? Is it working?

In other words, you are asking him to pour out his troubles into your ear. Out comes a vital essence for you: what the buyer NEEDS to address his problems. The gap in the market. It's a good idea to nod wisely or smile in sympathy and shut up thereafter, waiting until another occasion to pitch your actual project. It will then seem to 'miraculously' fit his needs.

The Magic Wand
Can be used in any situation or in conjunction with the above. It works well when your buyer is not articulating his needs in detail.

'Mr Executive, if you could wave a magic wand right now (over this project, over his slate), what would be the result?' This question, or words to the same effect, uncovers the key benefits he's hoping to get from you (or anyone, at this moment in time) – it could be higher ratings, big awards, press controversy, a certain actor, etc. I did this recently and realised that the project I was going to pitch would work better for the buyer if it were set outside London – he'd waved his wand and wished for 'regional' stories.

The Time Machine
Useful if someone is in a new job and trying to make their mark – or at the other end of the spectrum, heading for retirement.

'Mr Executive, if we move forward in time together two years from now, what films (or films featuring what talent) would you be launching at Cannes? In an ideal world, if a journalist was profiling your time here at X studio, what would you hope he would say?' As you can see, this is a sneaky way to ask them, 'What are you looking for?' but dressing it up as an adventure.

The Purchase Decision Ladder

Best used if the premise of the meeting is 'a general chat' – useful if the buyer is new to his job and defining his agenda to sellers. Needs about fifteen minutes to develop.

This interview technique is widely used by large corporations buying and selling billions of dollars worth of consumer goods such as toothpaste and soft drinks – and is easy to shift across to our industry. Write down all the factors your buyer considers when making an investment. With a soft drink, these might include price, carbonation, taste, calories, colour, packaging format, cost and so on. In films, we can include (without limitation):

> Screenwriter
> The Big Idea
> Genre
> Director
> Actors
> Slots/market
> Price /budget
> Setting
> Other

Before the meeting, rank these in order of importance to your buyer (your best guess). Then set them down in a vertical row on a piece of paper, placing the most vital factor at the top – so maybe you would put price or genre or director at the top of the 'ladder' and work on down from there. Then take your ladder picture to the buyer and bring him in on this little game. Ask him if he's got the time to help you gain a better insight into his decision-making process; I usually add here that I am trying to improve the targeting of my projects and development for him, 'so I don't waste your time submitting inappropriate material'. If he agrees, slide the page across to him and show him what you have *assumed*, asking him to correct it (move the rungs of the ladder around). In my experience, he will do so with alacrity. Through this process you not only demonstrate your great care for how he thinks (never a bad sign), but also learn much about his current criteria for buying. Some of it may be obvious, but there are always surprises. Also, this process can give you a deeper level of information about specifics: for example, once he has ranked 'actors', you might lean in and ask, 'What thoughts or ideas do you have about So-and-So?' Needless to say, this will help in your pitch thereafter.

I liken this exercise to squeezing water from a cloth – you can wring a huge amount of value from your buyer in a short space of time, and know that you are in synch with his mental processes long after you have left the building and the light has faded to black.

The last stop on our 'grand tour of the Buyer' takes us back to his exterior – and the perennially fascinating, controversial science of non-verbal signals.

Body Language

Some say this is not a science at all, and I can't claim to be an expert in the field. From talking to people who are, however, it's clear there is a good argument for some basic knowledge of the non-verbal 'clues' others give us when we meet them face to face. Also, in the last few decades, the study of body language has been refined and it has been adopted for use at all levels by big business around the world. If it's good enough for them, chances are we have something to learn. For our pitching purposes, here is a brief run-down of some of the key elements – you will soon see, at very least, why selling face to face has a huge advantage over selling by phone.

There are three main aspects:

Body and limb movements

You may already be aware of obvious examples of this, such as the renowned 'legs crossed towards you equals attraction'. But more useful to you in a business meeting are the subtler signs you can read or give off yourself. For example, if you are pitching and you want to elicit an answer without being so blunt as to say, 'Well? Do you like it?', back up your final point by showing open palms, which apparently prompts people to respond as effectively as if you'd just asked them to do so. Another relevant hand movement: a buyer with palms down on the desk is signalling certainty – which may be negative or positive, depending on the context. Crossed arms are an even more useful indicator. Check this at your next pitch meeting: if the buyer begins the meeting with his arms crossed and then uncrosses them as it develops, that is a good sign. He is literally 'opening up' to you and your idea. If he keeps his arms crossed he is blocking – which is not good. So, as an experiment I have tried ruses to 'unblock' buyers, such as passing them something or touching their arm lightly, or even throwing my arms open (often people will unconsciously mirror each other at close quarters, so this can actually cause him to do the same). In short, you want the buyer to welcome you and your idea with open arms – experience has shown me that he's more likely to do so if his arms are not shielding him.

Eye contact

You need not stare meaningfully into your buyer's eyes during the whole pitch. It seems the inverted triangle between eyebrows and chin is the area to look at. If you talk while looking at someone's forehead they think you are arrogant – I think it unlikely you would try to sell your film staring at the buyer's forehead, but be mindful of this. After I learned about this, I was acutely aware of my own eyelines in pitch meetings. I also realised, when I was in buyer mode, that people usually did stray outside that 'face triangle' when they were nervous, ill-prepared or arrogant, and the affect on me was negative.

Posture and position

A bent posture evidently signals a buyer wanting to say no or a seller without conviction. Forward sloping posture is dominating and aggressive – not a good selling mode. It's important to make space between yourself and the buyer – at least two, if not four, feet away if possible. Bear this in mind when you are taking seats to pitch at a long boardroom table or in a room with a wide seating area.

'Grooming'

One of my favourite body-language hints concerns 'grooming' as a negative signal. Evidently, if your buyer is picking fluff off his jacket or otherwise grooming his appearance, even if he is saying positive things to you, the opposite is true: he is not liking what he hears. This is where we get into that grey area about the 'science' of body language – especially since other manuals more geared towards social settings talk about grooming as a sign of intense sexual attraction!

Overall, I'd say always take body language in context. (One buyer said to me in protest, 'Hang on, I kept my arms crossed in that meeting because I was cold!') Buyers are busy people and generally, in my experience, many of them say exactly what they mean in order to keep the meeting short – and do not need to be interpreted to this degree. The real use of body language to you is in becoming aware of some of the behaviours recommended for YOU, as part of a general attitude of self-knowledge in a sales pitch.

And on that note, the spotlight swivels from the buyer to you. Are you ready?

GIRL MEETS BOY, FALLS IN LOVE, GETS PREGNANT. OLD BOYFRIEND SHOOTS HER AND UNBORN CHILD AT THE ALTAR. GIRL BECOMES SAMURAI WARRIOR, EXACTS BLOODY REVENGE.

Five

Preparing Yourself

I go for a lot of walks and drink plenty of water to get the brain in gear
David Yates, Director, *Harry Potter V*

If you cannot pitch your story to an executive, why should you expect he or she to be able to pitch to his or her boss and beyond that to an audience in TV ads or trailers? Anything can be pitched, it just needs the same amount of dedication given to it as the script itself.
Nick Osborne, Mission Management, Los Angeles

Whatever you do, as you make your way to the pitch, remember that they are buying into *you* as well as your idea; you are selling who you are and how you are – as well as your creative ideas. This is true whether you are the writer, producer, agent or any otherwise related person. We've already learned that buyers, be they venture capitalists or film executives, want to do business with effective professionals. How can you convey this?

The simplest way to guide your personal preparation is to provide you with a list of Dos And Don'ts, culled from across the industry, and augmented by the 'regular guys' out there selling cars and toothpaste.

Do . . .

. . . list some likely questions

Do ... (cont.)

The day before, *make a short list of the questions you are afraid they will ask.* If you can't think what those might be, ask a ruthless friend or colleague. Some of my personal favourites include: 'Isn't that very like the next Scorsese film?' Or: 'Do you actually have a signed option on the book in place?' Or: 'Do they have to be Scottish?' Find the good answers for the questions you've posed. If you are going in as a team, consider who is the person best suited to answer the trickiest questions.

... project a professional image.

Nothing succeeds like the appearance of success. Make of this what you will, considering your own style and who you are meeting, and err on the side of caution – and comfort. You also don't want to distract people from the creative material. For example, take my red leather jacket. I do not wear it to pitch meetings. Its very brightness and fire-engine redness become a talking point and a distraction – diverting time and concentration which is better focused on the subject of the meeting. This means reasonably neutral colours and plain accessories: no T-shirts with wacky slogans, no distracting, sexy or outrageous footwear, headgear or jewellery. It may sound dead boring, but every moment that the buyer spends looking at your accessories is a moment lost for your project. In short, dress for the situation.

... arrive early

Get there at least five to ten minutes early, and let the PA or receptionist know you have done so. It builds up subtle Brownie points with the buyer's support team if you impress them – good timekeeping helps to make their life easier when they are the gatekeeper of a busy diary.

. . . smile!

Greet the buyer with a smile and eye contact.

. . . put your pitch on paper

Write down the main points of your pitch on an index card (more on this to follow). You may not have to refer to this during the meeting, but it is a security blanket. There is no harm or shame in having it there. Please don't unfurl a big notebook from your voluminous bag, stuffed with bits of notes that keep fluttering to the floor. And when the buyer starts to give feedback, don't scribble notes furiously, turning pages like a concert pianist on speed. Buyers, like anyone else, are flattered if you note down their wise observations, but become nervous if they think you are writing down their every word.

. . . tell the truth

If you don't actually have the book option signed, what do you have? Have you spoken to the agent, got verbal permission to mention the book in this context? If it is like another film that's just been announced, how might you spin that? For example, using what advertising execs call 'the bandwagon technique', I might respond to the Scorsese question with the answer: 'Yes, it's a topical subject, everyone's climbing aboard – it's just in the zeitgeist at the moment. Of course, in *our* film, the twist is . . .'

'Tell the truth' would be my advice; although I remember when production funds fell through and I was forced to try

Do ... (cont.)

and salvage *The English Patient* by visiting all the Hollywood
studios with a briefcase full of cast photographs and location
shots. 'A strange man tries to remember who he really is
while recovering from terrible burns in the care of a
depressed French-Canadian nurse in a Tuscan monastery.
Then he dies.' Nobody wanted to make that movie.

Anthony Minghella, writer/director, *The English Patient*

... remember it is okay to say, 'I don't know'

You might be well prepared, but they might still surprise you
with a reaction from left field. It is perfectly fine – and indeed,
garners respect – to reply, 'Good question, and I don't have
the answer today. I'll come back to you (tomorrow/next
week) with some ideas on that.'

... programme yourself

Just before you go in to pitch, dwell on a recent success. Relive it
for a minute. The mind is a powerful tool and this simple trick
will position you to be confident. An extension of this is known
as 'Timeline Therapy' and is used by business practitioners of
neuro-linguistic programming. The simple principle is that we
can 'quick-fix' ourselves by training our brains to be positive,
based on our cumulative experience. Try this the night before a
pitch. Draw an imaginary line across the floor. Stand at one end.
At the other, imagine the door to the buyer's office. Now, in your
mind's eye, place on the line in front of you one of your achievements to date. This might be completing your first script, getting an agent, making a film, starting your own company,
winning a major award. Set down another one. And another.
Put at least half a dozen, like road markings along that imagi-

Do . . . (cont.)

nary line. They might not all be professional: you might include having a child, getting married or buying your house. Now, stand at the start of the line and walk it slowly all the way to the end, allowing yourself to feel the pride of each of your landmark achievements along the way. When you get to the end, throw open the door to the buyer's office (in your mind's eye) and say, 'Hello'. You will be exuberant, confident and ready to make a sale. Ever since I first heard this, I try to imagine that line (mine is always yellow) as I am led down the hall to the executive door. It certainly reverses any sense that I am heading towards my own execution, and gives me the ability to open strongly.

. . . have hope but not expectation
Remember, anything is possible.

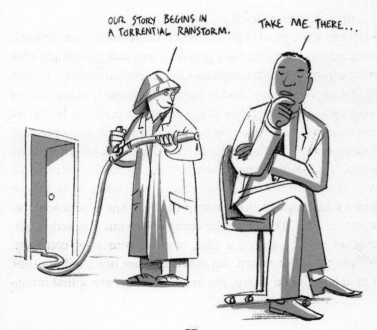

Don't . . .

. . . use gimmicks

In order to appeal to a select group of financiers we decided to have handsome small coffins (more like script-sized cigar boxes) made to send the script in. They each had a small plaque on the outside, a script laid in red velvet and a witty, funeral-type announcement. One of these packages was sent to Ricardo Mestres, then president of Hollywood Pictures, on the very day he got fired. He must have really wondered what else the day had in store for him after getting his pink slip and then this kind of 'voodoo doll' pitch from London!
Paul Trijbits, Producer, *Roseanna's Grave*, and Head of UK Film Council's New Cinema Fund

. . . light up a cigarette

I'm not your mother but allow me this one: *Don't smoke.* Obviously not *in* the meeting, but not even within an hour or two beforehand. Everyone associates smoking with fear – a billion-dollar subliminal advertising business is built on the back of this principle. By coming into a pitch meeting smelling of smoke you might as well have a note on your forehead stating: 'I am afraid'.

. . . apologise

It's very British saying 'Sorry' all the time, but others do it too. As in: 'Sorry, it's only a rough first draft, but hope you will read it anyway.' Or: 'Sorry, the idea isn't fully worked out yet.' Walk tall; be proud of your idea.

... pitch over the phone

Nothing is worse than trying this and hearing the other person tapping at their computer while you pour out your heart and soul. Much better to use the phone as a means to get a meeting.

... crowd the meeting

Consider the room size and the number of buyers. Nominate your key pitch team, which I suggest is ideally two people and in any event not more than three. If there's a large group of you involved, as can be the case, be ruthless. Your co-producer may be great creatively, but painfully shy; leave him at home. Your director may be a very witty raconteur; your writer may not be. Let the director start the meeting with a great story about why he got involved. In other words, play to your strengths.

... ramble

Try not to regurgitate the plot of the film in detail. Stick to the melody of the story.

... interrupt

Avoid cutting across the buyer or your teammates while they are speaking.

... cause offence

Do not offend the buyer by using blasphemy or bad language, or by criticising the competition.

or something you can't deliver

...ating comparisons

...tion other films that yours is like if they were
...e box office.

...mber pitching to adapt the sci-fi book *Spares* for
...amworks a few years ago. I started off gushing as usual
about how much I loved the material. Within seconds, I
pointed out that this could even be a second *Blade Runner*.
There was a long pause and then a very polite response: 'We
were thinking of it more along the lines of *Terminator 2*.' The
pitch ended very soon after. The other film I always rave
about, before being reminded it was a huge flop at the US
box office, is *Once Upon a Time in America*. The moral of the
story is: check your grosses before you enthuse.
Hossein Amini, screenwriter, *Wings of the Dove*

... 'carpetbag'.
In the aftermath of the American Civil War, opportunists
known as 'carpetbaggers' swept through the South stuffing

anything they could loot into bags made of old carpets torn from the floors of burnt-out mansions. They then sold the loot far and wide, hawking precious heirlooms as if they were meaningless: 'Two candlesticks for a dollar, four for the price of one, ma'am.' This image always comes to my mind when someone pitching to me dumps an indiscriminate pile of stories on my desk. While you may want one back-up up your sleeve at a pitch meeting, don't dump ten projects on the table just because they didn't leap at the one you really came to sell.

. . . abuse the 'X meets X' formula

As in 'This is *Titanic* meets *Ben Hur*.' Although I accept that this is a kind of industry-wide shorthand, personally I'd like to stamp it out, at least when it is used lazily and wrongly. It has become a cliché in Hollywood, but many Americans I have recently polled admit that it's not always effective. Wherever you may be, I suggest it is dangerous. You assume too much: namely that the buyer has seen both films, liked both and that both made money. Also, that the buyer has the wit to figure out why your film is a neat cocktail of the two X's. You're plunging on, describing your original story, while he's lost in reverie, thinking, 'I didn't see *Ben Hur*, but I know it had horses in it. So – what, the horses go to the sea and sink? Or fall in love across the social divide?' By the time you've retrieved his attention, you've lost the sale. A wise buyer friend of mine suggests that there is one particular time and place to use 'X meets X' pitching – indeed, where it may be expected of you. He advocates its use in the least creative, most 'business-only' situations – such as talking to a hard-nosed sales agent in a two-minute meeting at Cannes – rather than, for example, in an initial writer pitch with a creative producer. His reasoning is sound: some buyers take in 'X meets X' without great thought, and it helps them to do a kind of movie algebra. They take the two grosses and mentally combine them as you speak; so, taking the example of *Pretty Woman* meets *Out of Africa* – made famous in the first moments of Robert Altman's *The Player* – both of them are huge films. Not only do they exemplify their genre, involve major talent and have a certain genre-defining status, they also immediately resonate with profit. So the buyer's calculator goes 'X plus Y equals Z': that is, the combined gross of the films you just pitched will be the total gross of your new project. I'm prepared to believe there's a logic in that – but once again, I advise you that this form of pitching can backfire.

David Puttnam would describe his new project as a cross between *Citizen Kane* and *The Battle of Algiers*. I tried this myself with a script of mine which I described as 'a cross between *Dr Zhivago* and *The Last Emperor*'. To which the studio executive across the desk replied, 'Yeah, but what if it ends up being a cross between *Ishtar* and *Howard the Duck*?' Alan Parker, Director, *The Commitments*.

Now it's time for the meat and potatoes: the main course of your pitch is the project itself.

Six

Preparing the material

You have either a storyline or a script which you are going in
to pitch. Even if they have already read it, nine times out of
ten the buyer will ask you to 'tell it to me fresh' or 'give it to me
again'. So be ready, as if you are starting from a blank sheet of
paper with them. There are three bits of homework you can
do beforehand:

The résumé

Write down the beginning, middle and end of your story, giving just one line to each part – just ONE! This is a useful exercise for any writer or producer. If you are going in together
and the agreement is that the producer is going to lead the
pitch (very often the case), it can be fascinating for the writer
and producer to do this bit of homework separately and then
compare notes. See if you concur over what is of course the
same script, but which may be seen in different ways by the
team.

This will prepare you for a quick résumé of the story which
you may use at the end of the meeting; it will also shore up
your teamwork. I once heard screenwriting guru Robert
McKee memorably advising a young writer who wondered if
the producer he'd met was the right man for his project.
McKee said, 'Kid, a producer is only a guy with your script
under his arm. Get him to pitch it back to you to see if he's
read it right.' Even as I bristled with producer's antipathy, I

knew this was excellent advice – and have applied it often
since then as a producer, asking the financier what film he
thinks I'm making for him!

The USP
List your Unique Selling Points. You will remember how
important this is in the Investor's Quiz. In preparing your
USPs, you are not only identifying them but weaving them
into your pitch. So if you say, 'My title is *On Mars* and is the
exclusive true story of the first man ever to visit Mars,' that
weaves your USP into your story explanation. USPs are just
what they sound like: those distinguishing features that set
your project apart from the others. So what are those qualities in your film project?

At the obvious end of the spectrum, it could be that you have a piece of talent involved which is big-name: Brad Pitt is certainly a USP. So is 'based on a true story', as above. It might be that you've created the first horror-romantic comedy hybrid. And you're planning to shoot it on some new kind of stock which will give it a ground-breaking look,or it's all set underwater, or . . . whatever it may be, your project should have at least three USPs. This is both an art and a science – don't worry if you are having trouble identifying what they are.

It may help to ask yourself these questions:

Do you have well-known talent (director, actor, writer) attached?

Do you have underlying material (a book or play, for example) which has been a proven success already? (Have those figures handy)

Is your subject matter the star – often the case with British films? So is it a hot topic in the news, inspired by a tabloid event, etc?

Is there significant finance already in place or guaranteed to come because of some element? (casting/sponsorship opportunities/regional subsidy/etc)

Have you reinvented a genre? (A thriller starring children, for example, or a romance set entirely in space . . .)

Can you make it very cheaply (and well)?

At Coca Cola, one of the leading brands on the planet, they

have a neat trick. If, when defining their brand, they come up with a USP proposition – say, 'Coke quenches your thirst' – they substitute the word 'Pepsi'. If the sentence still makes sense ('Pepsi quenches your thirst'), then the SP is not U . . . and they kill it. Which is why their long-term tagline 'Coke is the real thing' works: it refers to the fact that Coke is the original soft drink, invented long before Pepsi. If you can substitute the words *Bend It Like Beckham* when highlighting the USP of your English football film, it's not a USP.

Another good exercise is to go for a drink with a friend who knows nothing about the project; ideally, a friend you admire and harbour a sneaking envy of, someone you'd like to impress. Tell them about the project. You will automatically put your best foot forward, especially if you are trying to hold their attention in a noisy bar. The first two or three points you make will naturally contain your USPs.

Finally, bear in mind that the USP is for the customer, not for you – these three key qualities should address the needs of your buyer and their buyers (the film audience out there). In other words, 'this is the best film I have written yet' is not a USP. It is for you . . . but not for them.

The PFC

Now prepare what I call the PITCH FORMAT CARD (PFC). Using this card will transform all your pitches from here on in – I have seen it happen! This is the nearest thing to 'pitch magic'. In effect, you are taking your story and pouring it through a strainer – you will capture the essential elements, the tealeaves rather than the whole cup of tea.

66

Take a big index card or half a sheet of A4 (in other words, don't give yourself too much space). Have your project firmly in mind. Now write down the following, in this order:

TITLE
GENRE
TIME AND PLACE
PROTAGONIST
HIS GOAL
OBSTACLES
RESOLUTION /WHAT'S LEARNED

Every story you could wish to tell can probably be reduced to this – even if you find it a bit of a struggle. I have heard any number of long-winded, oddball stories from a wide range of talent, and have directed them how to pour their genius through the simple sales 'sieve' of The PFC . Out comes a presentation both pithy and presentable which any buyer can judge on its own merit. I will expand further in a moment.

But first, bear in mind that most buyers will know if they even want to continue having the meeting after you have given them just the first *four* elements above. I unwittingly experienced this Law of Four for many years before I read that it was, in fact, one of the cardinal laws of selling: a buyer makes up his mind after only four key product elements become clear.

Usually one of these is major and three are minor. (One sales book I read called the major factor 'the hot button' – a term that sits nicely in the showbiz lexicon.) You'll witness this in action when you go out to pitch. Particularly with the most commercial buyers (such as sales agents or US studio execs). At the sharp end of where they live, they have a clearly defined competitive mandate which supports their brand. That hot button might be the hero, plain and simple. Disney will not buy a film with a protagonist who is a child molester. It may be genre for others. BBC Films are unlikely to back a teen horror flick. In short, the buyer may know if 'this is not for us' about one minute in. If you have done your homework about the pitchee's brand in advance, you will never stumble over those first few PFC items. If you haven't, you will fail.

Title

Film titles are best at one or two words. If not, the chances are they are adaptations, or everyone just shortens them – *Eternal Sunshine* being one example. Often long or complicated titles are there for insecure producers to hide behind.
Paul Brett , Prescience Film Financing

You'd be amazed how many pitchers neglect to state the title, so keen are they to get to the story. Surely your film has a title. If not, come up with a working title for it and always state it right at the top. A marketeer par excellence that I know offers up a great, if ruthless, test of a good title: the Box Office Moment. Let's say your film is a Swedish art house co-production called *Walking Through the Darkest Leaves*. Imagine you are at the box office of your local cinema. Try saying, 'Hi, two tickets for *Walking Through the Darkest Leaves*, please.'

How does that sound to you? If you find yourself stumbling over it, or in your mind's eye the box office attendant says, 'You mean *Wading Through the Dampest Breeze*?' you need to rethink. For one thing, nobody wants to be corrected at the box office, especially not with their date standing next to them. Even if it will almost certainly change ten times as you go down the development road, the first thing you are offering the buyer is this, your title. They know that it is the first thing the audience tune in to – up there on the marquee, or in the listings magazine, the title must 'speak to them'. A difficult and highly subjective game, but one that requires real thought before you pitch. If it comes to it, tell them it's untitled at the outset (without apologies); this is better than a bad title.

Genre
This is a French word meaning 'type'. What type of film have you got for us today? Is it funny, scary, thrilling, incendiary, romantic, horrifying? Does it *have* a genre? Many European filmmakers disdain the very idea: I have heard countless writers in the UK and Europe saying, 'I refuse to put my story into some *box*' – but the fact is, in a box is increasingly how films are sold. Walk into your local video and DVD shop tonight if you don't believe me. There you will see many videos and DVDs on shelves, each shelf neatly labelled: Comedy, Adventure, Thriller etc. Believe me, your buyer has to care an awful lot about genre. Even if you need to hyphenate the description three times, try to fill in this blank. In doing so , you may point out to them that you have created your own hybrid genre, or cannily point to a growth area in an unsung genre, such as children's horror, for example.

Place and Time
London, now . . . Outer Space, the future . . . Vienna, 1906. This is easy. If your film takes place in lots of places (*James Bond*)

and time scales (*The Hours*), you might just say, 'The time is the present day – the setting is London, Barbados and Red China . . .' or 'We are in New York and England, in three periods over the last century'.

Protagonist

Without something special in the characters, we won't care about the story whether it takes two minutes of our time or two hours. If you know more about your protagonist's car than his life – or his car is more interesting than he is – you're not ready to pitch his story.
David Howard , Director of Graduate Screenwriting, USC

Here I want to know, in the following order, his or her *name*, *gender* (if not obvious from the name), *age*, *job* and a few *intriguing short phrases* or adjectives to describe them. Nothing more. Why? Because, for many films and most buyers, this is the critical point: they cast the film in their heads. If you tell me, 'Our hero is James Bond, a debonair but deadly Englishman in his early forties who works as an international spy,' I've got the picture. And I can immediately start casting in my mind.

I am often asked what to do if it's an ensemble film. Even in an ensemble film there is a protagonist – witness, for example, Kevin Kline in *The Big Chill* or Hugh Grant in *Love Actually*, to name but two. On balance, these characters experience the most conflict in actual screen time. That is a good way to figure out who your lead is, just for the purposes of an initial pitch. I suggest also that the phrase or adjectives you choose should be appealing and/or intriguing: 'debonair' beats 'deadbeat' every time. That's not to say every protagonist is Bond – far from it – but as my mother always says, 'Tell me, what's to like?'

His Goal

What does he want? In *Lord of the Rings*, Frodo wants to deliver the ring. In *Titanic*, young Jack wants to find adventure on the high seas and get to America. In *Gladiator*, Maximus wants to avenge his family's death and get home. In *Bridget Jones*, she wants to find Mr Right. What does your hero want at the end of his travels? Is it love, revenge, escape, success? In other words, why are you putting him or her through some hundred-odd minutes of conflict and adventure – what is the point?

The Obstacles

What is stopping him or her from reaching that goal? Generally speaking, if you're making a full-length film, quite a lot. Here I would suggest you list as bullet points at least two or three big things that are in the way of your hero and success. If the answer is nothing, you're making a very short film. In *Lord of the Rings*, there's an obstacle a minute, whether in the form of evil creatures or forces of nature. In *Titanic* . . . for starters, there's an iceberg.

Resolution

What happens in the end? Again, you would be amazed how many pitches omit to mention this. We have already noted earlier that, according to our straw poll, this is one of the questions most commonly asked by buyers; let's eliminate it from your next pitch meeting. I have also been asked many times if describing the resolution is, in fact, counter-productive – if buyers know the end, surely they won't bother to read the script you want to give them after the pitch? Rest assured, I don't mean mechanically talking the buyer through every plot detail in the last ten pages of your film – you can leave some room for discovery, some tantalising sense of mystery. A simpler way to put this is: does he reach his goal? We know what that goal is – you just said it – so loop back to it and tell us, does he *get* love, revenge, escape etc? He doesn't have to, of course. Or he might get revenge, but also get killed (*Gladiator*). It need not be tidy. Within this round-up it is vital to explain what the protagonist, and the audience, learn from the journey you've sent them on. A film without epiphany is an empty vessel. However you perceive it, even at idea stage, you must tell the buyer what is learned. I have a writer friend who actually writes down his story outline using the word 'realises' as a linking device between each plot point: so, 'Joe is very shy but *realises* he'd like to marry. He meets Susan and soon *realises* she's the one. But then he learns she is dying, and he *realises* he must find the courage to declare his love before it's too late. In the end we learn, and he learns, that it is important to 'seize the day' when it comes to matters of the heart.'

Faced with the necessity to present the resolution in a compact fashion, writers might object, 'But this leaves out my whole second act.' That's right, pal, it does. Because this PFC is just the worm at the end of the fish-hook. If they nibble and bite, you can reel them in. This is not the end of the meeting, it is only the beginning.

```
┌─────────────────────────────────────────────┐
│              THE PFC                        │
│                                             │
│  TITLE                                       │
│  GENRE                                       │
│  TIME AND PLACE                              │
│  PROTAGONIST                                 │
│  HIS GOAL                                    │
│  OBSTACLES                                   │
│  RESOLUTION/WHAT'S LEARNED                   │
│                                             │
└─────────────────────────────────────────────┘
```

Example of a PFC

TITLE: *Bridget Jones's Diary*, (USP) based on the best-selling novel

TIME AND PLACE: Set in London now

GENRE: Romantic comedy, (USP) a contemporary *Pride and Prejudice*

PROTAGONIST: Bridget, scatty, endearing single girl in the big city

GOAL: She wants to find love and fulfilment

OBSTACLES: She's hooked on her boss, to be played by Hugh Grant (USP), a terrible cad who will never commit to her; also, her own insecurity about her looks and her place in the world; and the fact that Mr Right is obscured behind a terrible home-made jumper

Resolution/what's learned: In the end she does get together with Mr Right and learns that love is often right in front of you if only you could see it; we learn that the course of true love never did run smooth (again!)

ACT THREE

DELIVERY

Seven

Let's do it

How long should a pitch be?

I have a very low tolerance threshold personally when I'm listening to a pitch, and most execs I know are overwhelmed with material, so concise, smart and intriguing are my watchwords.
Colin Vaines, EVP, European Production and Development, Miramax/The Weinstein Company

Ten minutes. No more. Make it razor sharp.
Marion Rosenberg, Hollywood agent

Just as long as it takes to get the script read.
Stewart Till , Chairman, UIP

Tell them it's going to take less than five minutes, then watch their eyes as you get into it.
Richard Holmes, Producer

Every screenwriter knows the classic dramatic structure of three acts. My father, a successful pharmaceutical salesman for forty years, understandably didn't know this until I told him. He was mightily amused. 'We have three acts in selling too,' he told me. Subsequently I saw this little ditty in many sales manuals, but at the time I thought my brilliant dad made it up. Here it is:

Act One. Tell 'em what you're gonna tell them

Act Two. Tell 'em

Act Three. Tell 'em what you just told them, with a call to action

I often read magazines in the bathtub. I sink back into the bubbles and open *Vogue* or *Vanity Fair* with a happy sigh, only to sit up cursing as a pile of little sales handouts comes cascading out of the middle of the magazine into the water. After hearing the above 'Sales Structure', I took a closer look at these. To my amazement I saw that they all followed my dad's pattern.

'Get our Visa card and save hundreds of pounds!' trumpeted the facing side. Below that would be a detailed list of how that was going to happen, including collecting Air Miles, supermarket loyalty points, cashback and 0 per cent interest for the first six months. Overleaf was a summary which essentially reiterated, 'See – you can save hundreds with this Visa card!' And then – you guessed it – a call to action. Usually there's a form to fill out or a number to call. *Voilà!*

As you know, I am not averse to borrowing and adapting a tried and tested idea which might help us all pitch better. Even though a pitch meeting is a live, fluid interaction and never wholly predictable, it is certainly my experience that such a meeting can follow a rough three-act structure. That is, once you wade through some preliminaries (chats about the weather and digressions about industry politics or sport, for example) and tip into the actual pitch. From then on, there is a regularity and a rhythm to the process. It goes like this:

After the chit-chat, the buyer gives you a cue to get started.

I once walked into a pitch meeting with a studio executive that began just as I was taking off my coat. 'Go!' he said, glancing up. I nearly walked out – I thought he meant 'Leave'!

You are now in control of the shape of at least the next several minutes. Here's a simple outline of what happens next :

> Act One. Enthuse
> Act Two. Motivate/Persuade
> Act Three. Activate

ENTHUSE

PAT PAT!

Act One: Enthuse

My only advice on pitches is: keep them very economical, open with something that holds the listener's attention, and if you're leaving a script or a synopsis behind, don't try to tell the whole story – far better to leave people dangling and asking to know what happens next, at which point you can leave them with other material. I once pitched a project which was a book on the basis of a proposed opening scene, which I made intriguing enough for the company to read the book and get involved. In the script, the opening scene was entirely different!

Colin Vaines, EVP, Production and Development, Miramax/The Weinstein Company

Every salesman in the world will tell you to 'open strongly'. The winning pitch team for the Sydney 2000 Olympic bid opened its bid to the assembled committee by turning off the lights and firing a starter pistol. That got their attention. Stories of mad American pitches abound – producers opening the meeting by bringing in actors, lighting effects and even large zoo animals to aid their cause. One story I heard had a team of army commandos abseiling down the side of a major US network's headquarters in order to alight on the windowsill of the room where the producer of a major new adventure series was in full flow. I am doubtful whether these tricks would work in Britain, or indeed Europe, where attention-seeking is likely to be more conversational. Depending on the story you've come to sell, your gambits might include:

• Ask a question ('Do you remember your first love?'; 'Did you know that a guy lived in Paris airport for seven years?')

• Mention a hot topic in the headlines ('One in two marriages end in divorce today.')

• Make a surprising statement – tell them something they don't know ('Aliens are living among us.')

By now you should have their attention. Now do them a favour – give them something.

TELL 'EM WHAT YOU'RE GONNA TELL THEM. Don't get into the detail yet, just set it up: 'We're here today with the ideal Christmas movie for you'; 'I've come across the most remarkable true story for a romantic comedy.'

DEMONSTRATE YOU'VE DONE YOUR HOMEWORK ABOUT THEM AND THEIR COMPANY. You can slip this in quite easily: 'As Londoners, we are constantly up against the problem of . . .' or 'Having had such success recently with fact-based drama, you'll know there's an appetite for this genre.'

Also within this opening section you can:

• Establish how much time you've got (if that is not clear upfront)

• Introduce any colleagues (director/writer) you've brought with you

• Make sure you are clear on the different buyers' names (and try to use them in subsequent conversation, as a mark of respect)

By the time you are through Act One, your buyer will feel primed and ready to listen to the detail, having had the scene set for them by someone who has established respect and a certain common ground. As a buyer, I feel such gratitude to the seller who gives me the big picture first before plunging into the detail. It's like finding your seat in the cinema, getting the popcorn out and relaxing into the main event – very gratifying.

MOTIVATE/PERSUADE

Act Two: Motivate/Persuade

Why motivate? Frankly, you are motivating the buyer to stay tuned in to you, to keep listening when he's got a million things on his mind and a busy day behind or ahead of him. You are, of course, also motivating him to want what you are selling and persuading him to get interested: to ask questions, to make a contribution to the meeting. It is in this section that you 'tell 'em' – so here you give them the content of your pitch. This is where your precious PFC comes into play. The essential items on that card, as well as your Unique Selling Points, make up the body of Act Two. Get them all out there – title, time and place, genre, protagonist etc – and then stop. When you reveal 'how it ends and what is learned' you've said enough – just for the moment. Now shut up and listen while they start to question you.

Their questions and your answers make up the rest of Act Two, which may last five minutes (you present your core idea, they reject it) or more than an hour. Once they start participating, I'd say as a general rule 'the longer the better'. I tend to judge how well a pitch meeting has gone by how long Act Two lasted. All the while you are motivating and persuading them, if only to ask more questions, which keeps the story 'alive' between you. If a buyer is asking a lot of detailed story questions in a pitch meeting and even suggesting some changes and ideas of his own, you've got him on the hook. So keep him talking. Don't interrupt, and if he solicits your input on one of his story points, make sure to start each response with words to the effect of 'good question' or 'that makes sense' – or, if necessary, 'I don't follow you: can you elaborate on that?'

Producers are just like writers in at least one respect – they like their own ideas better than anyone else's ideas. If you give a pitch that is so ironclad that it forbids input from a producer, they are less likely to want to pursue your project than one that allows them room to contribute their ideas. Leave room in your pitch to be helped with the story.
David Howard, Head of Screenwriting, USC

At the end of Act Two you will have a strong sense of what the buyer makes of your project and whether you are in with a chance or not. If things have gone badly, and it's clear they don't want your project, now is the time to abandon that ship with grace and try to wind up the meeting by asking for a few more moments of their time to try some of the more general questioning tools outlined earlier: the

Ladder, the Pain Funnel or the Magic Wand, as you see fit. No pitch meeting is wasted, even if the project itself goes unsold!

If things have gone at all well, it is very likely that they will be making 'okay, let me read it/go away and think about it/talk to colleagues' noises at this point. We now move into Act Three.

ACTIVATE

Act Three: Activate

Act Three is pretty brief. It's a chance to summarise and make the 'call to action' – what you'd like them to do next. First of all,' tell 'em what you just told them.' I often use the phrase (and you will find your own words): 'So basically it's a [romantic comedy for kids, or whatever]' – usually the same phrase I used to set it all up back in Act One. Then I give them the three-line summary from my preparatory homework. This might be as brief as 'Boy meets girl. Boy goes on safari with girl and saves her from lions. Boy gets girl.' If you are wary of repeating what you said just a few minutes earlier, don't be. Selling is a repetitious game, it's meant to be (remember those little adverts that fall out of magazines?), and don't worry – it works! Part of what you are doing here is imprinting the project and its basic 'logline' on their brains, so that they can repeat that line to their boss and colleagues later on. If you give them a good strong baton to pass on, this is incredibly persuasive.

Secondly, agree on the next step or 'task', both for you and the buyer. So – are they going to go away and read the script? Are you meant to ring again in two weeks/bring in the director/find out if that actor is available/interested and let the buyer know? In what time scale? This is a form of persuasion too: you are asking them to collude with you and move the story on.

While all this is being agreed, STAY IN YOUR CHAIR. For some reason, pitchers are always very eager to get out of the door after Act Two. It must be relief. Then they realise they haven't worked out what to do next , and stand hovering in the doorway, the noise of the office outside pouring in and drowning out these vital final words. The meeting ain't over 'till it's over. Stay in your chair, do the call to action, then thank them for their time. Then and only then is the pitch meeting at an end.

Eight

Out in the cold

What happens if you can't get into the pitch meeting room in the first place?

There are two other kinds of pitch you can undertake:

Written: the sales letter
Opportunistic: the informal pitch

The sales letter

I can look at the envelope and tell you that it's good. It just vibrates
Stephen Frears, Director, *Mrs. Henderson Presents*

Again, tomes have been written on this subject. My favourite quote is: 'a sales letter is just you in an envelope'.

Do not underestimate the power of a sales letter. It can be as personal and persuasive as a live pitch. It should follow the same three acts: enthuse, motivate and persuade, with a call to action.

Your letter should sound like natural speech – avoid expressions like 'as per' or 'please find enclosed'. Make sure it is laid out on the page in an appealing way. Avoid one large block of prose: you might use bullet points and varying paragraph widths as a visual gimmick to hold the reader's attention.

Once you've composed the letter, try the Grab Test. Give it to a colleague, ask them to read it, count to five and then grab it back. If they can't tell you what the letter was about, you failed.

Do . . .

Type the letter and sign it yourself
Know your goal for the letter (a meeting, a script read?)
Get spelling, syntax, grammar, names/job titles right
Keep sentences short – ten to twenty words maximum
Suit the style and tone to the reader's knowledge of you
Use CAPS, <u>underlining</u>, **bold** and *italics* sparingly
Steal good lines from other people's letters
Stay accurate and truthful

If enclosing script, make it standard form (Final Draft)
Include a call to action at the end: 'Look forward to hearing from you soon' is a good one

Don't . . .

Use funky paper or typeface – this is a business
Cause offence through humour, sarcasm, irony, bad language, blasphemy etc
Run to two pages, no matter what!
Knock the competition
Fill the letter with empty overstatement ('fabulous', 'extraordinary')
Make excuses ('This is only a first draft' etc)
Enclose an SAE (if they can't afford postage, they can't

finance your film)
Include gifts, bribes, drawings etc.
Chase a reply before a month has elapsed

They say good sales letters are like poetry: every word has to count. Hone and revise, read aloud, hack out the dead wood. It is more than likely only half the letter will be read – and that very rapidly – so you have only seconds to make an impact. Here is an example of a bad sales letter:

Dear Sir or Madam
    I am writing to tell you about my screenplay which I have written or rather written half of and I am trying to find a producer or a home for it although I do not have an agent and I am not quite finished. ANYWAY!! I wonder if you would be so good as to read the enclosed pages, which I have written by hand as my 8*&%$£ computer is always crashing (!!!) and it drives me nuts!! PLEASE, *please* read quickly as I have lots of people interested including Stephen Daldry to direct but I would like to know what you think. I am also very willing to come to see you in the next week to discuss your reactions and would be glad to do this for exampel at 2pm next Tuesday if you have the time, I am sure you will want to onceyou have looked at my fantastic script!!! I don't know if it is TV movie or a film btu myabe your company does both??! Well we will soon find out! Have a super day,

    Love, Bob. (SAE enclosed!)

And here is an example of a good sales letter:

Dear Eric

How many weddings have you been to this year? I'm guessing at least half a dozen. This has to be the most universal of experiences – for audiences everywhere, of any age. Richard Curtis, award-winning comedy writer of BBC hit *Blackadder*, has written the enclosed romantic comedy *Four Weddings and A Funeral*, which charts the progress of a handsome, commitment-phobic bachelor (think Hugh Grant) through a summer of weddings – and one funeral. Mike Newell is attached to direct and all rights are available. I urge you to read just the first few pages – and dare you to stop there.

Look forward to hearing from you,

Many thanks,
Bob

Opportunity knocks

I was pitched at a Sikh temple at a funeral service for a relative. I had to ask them to respect the dead relative and moved away relieved.
Gurinder Chadha , Director, *Bend It Like Beckham*

We've all been there. The one man who could green-light your film is suddenly right across the table from you at a dinner party. Or across a crowded room at a film festival. Or even in the lift with you in the tallest building in town. Like the babbling pitcher who dogs Tim Robbins' every step in the first sequence of Robert Altman's *The Player*, you can't stop yourself.

The Americans actually call this the Elevator Pitch – and

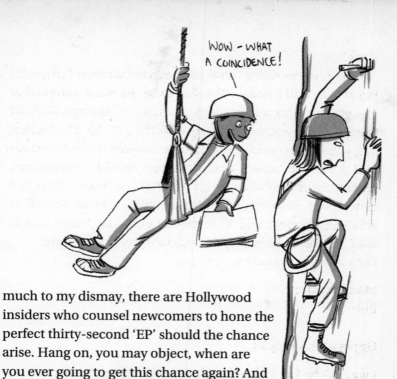

WOW – WHAT A COINCIDENCE!

much to my dismay, there are Hollywood insiders who counsel newcomers to hone the perfect thirty-second 'EP' should the chance arise. Hang on, you may object, when are you ever going to get this chance again? And in you launch, talking fast because the lift is already at Floor Four and going fast – and the buyer stands there, captive, perhaps nodding politely, maybe even smiling at you, but essentially HE IS DYING TO GET AWAY FROM YOU. I suggest you never do this – it is not the way to make a sale. So are you just going to let him get away? No, it's possible to make a quick, Scud missile-like strike, just a brief encounter which may set you up for a longer session another time. The lighter of touch and the more easygoing you are, the more likely you are to see this great contact in future. A few tips for the informal pitch:

Keep your conversation very general
As in: 'I am a screenwriter, Mr Bruckheimer, and I don't want

to trouble you here, but I have a thriller script set in the time of the Crusades which I thought would interest you – may I send it to your office?'

Make sure the time and place are appropriate
Don't take hostages at public events, cornering buyers and making them listen.

Stay clear-headed
Nothing will be relevant or worth following up later unless you and the buyer are both sober.

If possible, use someone else you both know to 'connect' you
This means that there's a credible link in the introduction – almost like using an agent to submit material. So when you follow up later, you can also say, 'You'll remember Tom introducing us at the party the other night . . .' – and who knows, maybe he will.

If possible, ask some exploratory questions
If you find yourself in the enviable position of having a seat next to a key buyer for some period of time, not just a few moments, try to use some of the questioning devices outlined earlier. The Time Machine is a good one, as is the Magic Wand. Both are kind of fun 'games' which allow the man to talk about himself and his concerns. Then just sit there and be a good listener. At the end of your light-hearted and easygoing chat (which I hope is not all about work), you can then ask if you may send him a script or come to see him 'some time' – don't be pushy, don't rush to pitch anything, even if he seems genuinely friendly by this time. This is show business, not show friends. Wait until he's back at work.

Nine

In The End

I want to thank everyone who spends part of their day creating. I don't care if it's a book, a film, a painting or a dance, a piece of theatre, a piece of music. Anybody who spends part of their day sharing their experience with us . . . I think this world would be unlivable without art.
Steven Soderberg, Oscar acceptance speech

Stories are how we all make sense of the world and share our experience. Shame on the people who say drama and films are not important, not 'saving lives' or not 'rocket science'! Telling stories to each other always has been, and always will be, vital. But if we don't know how to do it well, those stories stay hidden, locked in fertile imaginations or between cardboard covers – doomed to be 'Incomplete Works' for evermore.

Pitching is the link between your stories and the money to make them. While you cannot control how other people will react to your pitch, you can prepare and arm yourself. The final piece of preparation you should do before you sally forth, is this: be sure you know what you want out of the meeting. It's easier to know what you want if you have clearly stated it to yourself first. This may sound odd: surely, in any pitch meeting, we all just want to sell our ideas? But what is the *specific* outcome you need? You would be amazed at how many pitchers don't quite know what their goal is. What do you hope will have been gained (or moved towards) by the time you walk out of the building? This could include:

- Advice
- A creative partner (co-writer, for example)
- A co-producer
- A mentor (which may be a prerequisite of the financiers if you are new to the industry)
- Script money (how much)
- Production money (how much)
- Validation (for example, when a writer pitches to his agent)

You are the hero of your own pitch meeting. Establish what you want, what is stopping you from getting it, and what you need to overcome. In the end, whatever happens, you will learn (as I have done and continue to do) from every single pitch meeting you take – whether as buyer, seller or onlooker. There is always more to be mined, new angles to consider, in that relentless uphill struggle to shepherd a Big Idea from that wonderful 'Ping!' of inspiration to a screen near you.

If you:

Gather information on the market and buyer
Polish up your communication skills

And:

Remain true to yourself
Have passion and tenacity
Follow in the footsteps of others who have been successful at selling

you will give your Big Idea its best chance for success.

You may be familiar with the law of Cause and Effect, a resonant law in sales as in life. For every effect there is a cause. Pitching success is an effect. It has specific causes. All I've done here is find people, both within and without the industry, who are good at selling. My proposition was simple: if we do what they do, we'll get the same results. This is not a miracle, or good luck. Selling is simply a learned skill, based on information-gathering and communication skills. With the tools contained in these pages, and the talent to back it up, you can do anything.

Pitching is an art in itself. You may be a great writer but a lousy pitcher. Deal with it.
Marion Rosenberg, Hollywood agent

Please stay seated for a moment longer . . .

Call to Action

You may have bought travel guides from time to time which ask you for feedback about the hotels and attractions recommended therein – ratings or experiences you care to contribute which will make the journey better for future travellers, or perhaps tips for other sites you can recommend. We'd like to ask the same of you here, so that we can continue to update and improve *The Pitch* in future.

Name / Age / Nationality / Occupation

I have a pitch story for you: . . . .
. . . .
. . . .
. . . .
. . . .

I have an addition or modification to
Commonly Asked Buyer Questions:
. . . .
. . . .
. . . .
. . . .
. . . .

I road-tested one of the pitch tools (. . . .)
with the following result : . . . .
. . . .
. . . .
. . . .
. . . .
. . . .

I would like further information about pitch lectures in my
area – (provide details)

Please email us at rightpitch@hotmail.co.uk – and thank you
for your time.

In return, at the back of this book you will find your very own tear-out-and-keep PFC card for your pitch preparation – guaranteed for life to add clarity and brevity to any pitch. Good luck!

MIX TO:

I had flown into Paris that morning.

On the plane I had caught up with my reading. This had included the latest draft of Neil Jordan's latest script The Soldier's Wife. It was fantastic.

I was so excited by it I wanted to pitch it to the passport controller! But he was not interested. Then I tried the cab driver on the way in from Charles De Gaulle airport. He did not speak English.

As I entered the reception of (at that time) France's most active production company, I decided in my mind to try it with them. I had never pitched it before. I had no idea how I was going to pitch it.

I had not planned to do so. In fact I had arranged the meet with some difficulty. The assistant kept asking me what the meeting was about when I was trying to fix it up. I kept on saying that we had produced *Company of Wolves*, *Mona Lisa*, *Scandal*, *Absolute Beginners*, etc. but that I was not coming to pitch something. I had said I would just like to meet the head of production. It was, I said in a very British way, 'a get to know him meet'.

In that case, she suggested on the phone, I would I like you to take her boss out to lunch. That's how they do it in France she explained patiently.

I explained I was from Rock 'n' Roll and we did not do 'lunch' (big mistake!), I explained to her (having just seen the film *Wall Street*) that I did not have time for time consuming lunches, that lunch was for wimps! I think this rather perversely impressed her and she grudgingly gave me an appointment.

So here I was in reception about to see one of France's most maverick producers, of amongst others all the David Lynch films of the era. And here I was desperate to try pitching a film when I had sworn when making the appointment that I did not want to pitch anything!!

By now I was in his office, seated awkwardly across his desk (he had offered me the sofa but again I had perversely refused). I cleared my throat . . .

'The Soldiers Wife . . .' I began 'is set in Northern Ireland'

'Zat ees a negatif!' he interjected before I could get another word in.

'But it moves to London at the end of act one!' I almost shouted, upset that he had interjected before the end of my first sentence.

'Zat ees definitely sexier, London ees an interesting town!'

'City' I corrected him but then thought better of it and continued . . .

'A member of the IRA . . .'

'Vous mean ze freedom fighters??'

'No I mean the Irish Republican Army'

'Aaah! Zat is another negatif!'

'Ok . . . anyway' I continued . . . rather desperately now

'The Ira man kills a black British soldier'

'Zat iz not good . . .' he interjected again.

At least he did not say 'Zat is another negatif'!' I thought to myself. I spoke too soon.

'Zat is another negatif'

'Which bit is negative?' I asked mischeviously 'The soldier, the fact he is black or the fact that he gets killed?'

'Go on . . .' He said without answering the question.

So I continued less and less enthused.

'Well' I said, 'the IRA guy falls for the wife of the soldier he has killed whom he meets in London'.

'Aaah . . .'

'But', I said, 'there is a problem'

'What problem?'

'The wife, she is a man'

There is a long silence. One of those long hateful silences. One of those silences that says to me 'Nik, you have just delivered one of the worst (and unfinished!) pitches of your life'.

'This film ees full of negatifs . . . '

'I know that!' I shouted. 'You have told me enough times.'
('You stupid frog' I thought to myself)

The silence continued . . .

'BUT I LUV IT !!!!'

I almost fell off my chair in shock.

He did not finance the film but we did get a fantastic dinner
out of it!

Oh yes – and we changed the name of the film from The
Soldier's Wife to *The Crying Game*.

Nik Powell, Director, National Film and Television School,
London

THE PFC

TITLE

GENRE

TIME AND PLACE

PROTAGONIST

HIS GOAL

OBSTACLES

RESOLUTION/WHAT'S LEARNED

NOTES

NOTES

NOTES

NOTES

NOTES

NOTES

NOTES

NOTES

NOTES

NOTES

NOTES

NOTES

NOTES